Giving Birth to God

Karen Adler

Giving Birth to God

Acknowledgements

The cover image of *Giving Birth To God* is a composite photograph of the Clare Franciscan Monastery in Stroud, Australia, plus an image from the TV program *Stephen Hawking's Universe*.

The two images melded together reflect my view that we would do well to heal the divide between religion/spirituality and science, to allow one to complement the other rather than enduring an endless battle between powerful forces both of which contribute greatly to humanity.

Giving Birth to God
ISBN 978 1 76109 667 9
Copyright © text Karen Adler 2023
Cover image: Karen Adler

First published 2023 by
Ginninderra Press
PO Box 3461 Port Adelaide 5015
www.ginninderrapress.com.au

Contents

Giving Birth to God	7
All Around Her the Sun Danced	11
And She Kept Saying Goodbye	13
April Daze	14
The Art of Slow and Gentle Change…	16
Beauty Comes To Me	21
Beauty is only	22
Beware the Twisted Woman	23
Buff Underparts	24
Crowdreaming	27
Curse	29
Dark Imaginings	32
Dearall	35
Do Middle-aged Men Travel On Buses?	38
Down the Bunny Hole	39
Epidermic Growth	41
Fear is leaving now	43
Feet in the Sand, Head in the Clouds…	45
For God, King and Country	47
From the Shadow Lake	49
Ghosts of Christmas Past	50
Good Catholic Girls	51
Hardening of the Hearteries	53
Hardly Ever Drowning	54
He Sculpted Her In Sand	56
How	59
I Have Lived Long	61
I Have Seen People Create	62
I Painted the Sky Last Night	64
In the End Times	66

Just Because	70
Kissing You	72
Know & Tell	74
Minutes	77
My Secret Love of Spindrift	80
Ocean Mist	82
Pitcher Plants and Pitfall Traps	83
The Pheromone of Love Meets the Scent of Sex	86
Record Keeping	87
Pockets	90
Requiem for Eagles	91
A Small Kindness	93
Smatterings	95
Walking's Enjoyment is Three Level Vision	98
When Death Comes	100
A Woman and Two Candles	102
The Woman Called God	104

Giving Birth to God

I will wrap myself around the Earth
around the whole of the Earth
around her roundness.
I will feel the concave cavities
of her valleys
and the sharpness
of her mountains.

I will grow moist
from her seas and oceans
her rivers and lakes
her cool, clear streams.

I will feel the moisture
of her rainforests
and the dryness
of her deserts.

My skin will be wet
from droplets of water
that fly from rain-wet trees
whipped by wind.
My skin will be scorched
by the touch of hot sand.

I will wrap myself around the Earth
and I will look upon her with joy.
My senses will be inflamed
by the colours of the Earth –
by the silver scales of fish
that swim in her waters,
the vibrant beauty of flowers
that grow in her soil.

My senses will delight
in brown and red and golden leaves
that hang from bare branches
of wintertime trees.
My senses will soar
with the flight of rainbow birds
into clear summer skies.

I will wrap myself around the Earth
I will incubate her
and I will give birth to God.

I will be the womb
and the Earth will be the seed inside me.

Together, we will bear and birth a new God.
I will love and nurture the Earth
as I love and nurture myself.
I will feed her full of goodness
as I would feed a small and trusting child.
I will feel her grow happy
and strong
and content
inside the circle of my body.
And I will feel the seed of God
growing inside the Earth,
inside me.

I will wrap myself around the Earth
at the dawn of time
and during the dark night of the soul.
I will wait for days and nights
and suns and moons.
I will look inside myself
at the Earth's waters.
I will feel the quickening
of the Earth's heartbeat.
I will feel God growing within the Earth
and my soul will grow bright.
I will wait with patience
until God is ready to emerge
from my mating with the Earth.

And who will be the midwife at this birth?
Who will assist
with the birth of this new God
who rises from out of the Earth
rather than coming down from the sky?

I will choose old women
with strong hands
and old men
who tend fires on cold nights.
I will choose young women
who laugh with the joy of freedom
and young men who walk tall and proud.
Together, we will watch the sun rise;
together, we will see it set.

I will wrap myself around the Earth
and I will feed and protect and love her
and I will give birth to God.

I will wrap myself around the Earth
and I will give birth to God.

2000

All Around Her the Sun Danced

All around her
the sun danced with shadows
light
flickering fading
shadow absorbing light
light dancing out of shadow
escaping.

Shadow boxing
light and shadow
entwined grappling
supremacy attained then lost
old wounds
reopened
re-blooded.

All inside her
dark shadow
releases gifts
into the light
companioned by
putrid suppurating
stink-flesh
of old wounds
reopened
re-blooded.

Surfacing
from darkness into light
all inside her
opening up
blossoming
from deep diving
dark depths
into light dancing
all around her.

2017

And She Kept Saying Goodbye

And she kept saying goodbye
before it was really time,
before anyone had actually left,
because she had one foot out the door herself,
ready to leave before she was left,
ready to brush away the dust of footprints
of those who may be leaving,
who may be on their way,
before she herself was on her way,
as she said goodbye
before it was really time,
before anyone had actually left.

2000

April Daze

April daze
filling themselves
up to the brim
with moments
that pass –
passing you by moments.

And moments that arrive
without giving you
any notice at all –
rude moments of awakening,
uninvited guests moments.

April daze
brimful
of old dog demands
pulling us into
the dark days
of death and decay.

April daze
brimful
of old dog delights
in days spent
resting and recollecting
and weaving and connecting
old dog wisdom
with old dog knowing.

April morns and April dawns
April mourns the passing of March
and the march of passing people,
of friends and love that have passed
into the April daze
of my kind-hearted
sad-hearted friend
who has lived
her seventy or more
long meandering years
carrying within her
the imagination of a frightened child
of all things falling,
all things failing,
abandoning hope
all ye who enter here
all of she who enters here
abandoning ship
before even
the shipwreck.

She merges into
the dawning and the mourning
of her April daze
with her old dog sadness
and her old dog kindness.

2015

The Art of Slow and Gentle Change…

This art of slow and gentle change
    is artful
        but free from artifice
            is devoid of artificiality
                despises fakery.

This artist of change
    this change-maker
        she sees through the trickery of the Trickster
            silently observes the two faces of Janus
                avoids like the plague
            the mindfuckery of all the Toads toadying
        the washerwomen and the brainwashers
    who tootle through the countryside
delivering coals to Newcastle
    riches to the rich
        tax havens to the haves
            van lives to the have-nots.

This change-artist –
    she uses soft brushes
        made from spidersilk
            spun on webs that
                hold drops of rain
                    and catch flies
                        and capture moths
                  that shimmer in the light
                that hold the spiders
              that spin the spidersilk
        into webs.

This artist of slow and gentle change
    is slow,
    and she moves gentle
    swaying with the winds of change
    seeking shelter from the storm
    holding fast to the moment
    like a spider
        spinning her spiderweb
            spun from spidersilk
                that has the strength of tensile steel
                      and holds her with gentle
                          spidery hands.

The art of slow and gentle change
    is slow and serene
        is somewhat
            just slightly
                because experience has taught her so
            wary of the Ides of March
        the tides of the full moon
    lapping dangerous
at her door
    the ebbing and flowing
        of night into dawn into day into soft afternoon
            that circles back to night
                into dawn
                    into day
                        into soft afternoon.

This wiser-now artist
    tides herself over
    keeps her head
    while all about her are losing theirs
    she keeps hers above water
    senses the gentle lap of tides
    from primordial oceans
    from aeons ago
    and ages distant
    and from a galaxy far far away
    she feels the tables turning
    and the tides turning
    and the Earth's heart beating
    and the Earth's lungs breathing.

This wiser-now, older-now, stronger-now artist
    more-slow-now, more-gentle-now
    she sees herself and breathes herself
    through this change
    and keeps the wolf from the door
    the wolf with his sharp and shiny celebrity teeth
    and his wolfish grin
    artificial and full of artifice
    she keeps the door firmly closed
    no thank you, Mr Wolf, Mr Made For TV
    not by the hair of my chinny-chin-chin
    she bridges the gap
    between here and there
    between now and then
    and now

      and the new-now
          and the this-now
              and the past-now
                  and the future-now
              and the ever-present now
          and the now that is a circle
    and a spiral
forever spiralling out of control
      and then spiralling back
          to this poetic form
              this complex
                  weblike shape
                      of spiderwebs made from spidersilk
          …creating
        …and then destroying
      …and now creating
        …and now destroying.

This artist of slow and gentle change
    enjoys gentle afternoons
    and genteel evenings
    that fall softly
    like a curtain falling slowly
    on a stage
    on a life
    changing the light
    as the light changes
    and moves around the earth
    that moves around the sun
    and circles the moon

and back again
and spins
like a top
in deep space
and spins spidersilk
and births change
and is changeable
and change is lapping at the shore
of this morning.

2021

Beauty Comes To Me

Beauty came to me this morning,
beauty visited me through the night.

Is it only to my home
that beauty comes at the dawning?
Is it only my life
my world that beauty makes again so right?

Only in my bed
that the morning is so glorying?
Only on my day
this one fine bright and glorious day
that the beauty of light replaces the beauty of night?

Skin – this thin sliver of skin – that separates a promise from a warning,
skin – this merest fragment of flesh – that separates fight from flight.

Deep, down down deepest deep,
of this day's borning,
deep, deepest deep movings
of this soul's reaching for might.

2011

Beauty is only

Beauty is only as deep as your skin
as deep as the depths of my soul
gazing into the wide blue beyond
secreted inside that bottomless pool
of savage yearning
wanting
needing
madness
that hides beneath my wide-eyed
shunning
of the shallowness of your beauty
and the depths of my sadness.

2015

Beware the Twisted Woman

Beware the twisted woman,
she who calls herself friend.

I'd like to help in any way I can,
she says,
as she pushes all your buttons,
and pulls on strings,
as she plays puppet-master,
manipulating,
scheming,
as she systematically
spreads her poison.

Beware the twisted woman,
she with the black mark on her face
and blackness
in her heart and in her soul.

Pity the twisted woman,
wonder why
…but pass on by.

Forgive the twisted woman,
pity she with
the venom
running in her veins,
slowly poisoning her blood.

2013

Buff Underparts

The brush cuckoo,
similar in shape
to the pallid cuckoo,
has more buff underparts
than its sad and sorry colleague
of the pallid,
but no less valid,
variety.

There are many men
in this world of
underparts envy
who would wish
to emulate
the brush cuckoo
and have
more buff underparts
to call their own.

Buff underparts
do not appear,
however,
to have served
the brush cuckoo
particularly well.

Its call
is shrill,
far-carrying,
deliberate.
'Fear-fear-fear',
it cries into the bush
or in your back garden,
where,
being a nest parasite,
it has laid its eggs
in the nests
of small songbirds.

Which state of affairs
may go some way
towards explaining
why the brush cuckoo's call
becomes ever more shrill,
ever more demented,
crying repeatedly
into the existential void
from its hijacked nest,
'Where's the tea, Pete?'

A cuckoo in the nest
is an idiom
meaning an unwelcome intruder in a place
or situation.
No doubt,
this idiom originates
from small –
but articulate –
songbirds.

And we wonder why –
unnecessarily
it now seems to me –
we refer to
slightly crazy,
slightly mad people,
as 'cuckoo'.

The brush cuckoo
also sometimes collides
with lighthouses.

What the fuck brush cuckoo?

2015

Crowdreaming

The harsh cry of a single crow
cracks the stillness of early morning,
signalling the day to emerge
from its dark cocoon.

Other sounds follow on
and the world erupts into being,
full of noise and movement,
light and life.

I prefer the stillness,
the blackness of the night.
It's then that I travel
the pathways of my dreams,
daylight only serves to remind
that those dreams aren't real.

Or are they? I wonder
as I see the crow swooping above,
black wings glistening in sunlight.

A broken fragment of last night's dream
slices its way through the thin veil
separating night and day:
a black shadow figure,
flying high and crying harshly,
followed me through my dreams last night.

Trailing a filmy length of snow white gauze,
like a cloud wisp snatched from the sky,
the shadow guided my footsteps,
signalling where and when to stop.

1997

Curse

When the Wicked Fairy realised –
with that flash of blinding illumination
that comes
so swiftly
so suddenly
that it cuts clean through
her sweet and sickly
thinly veiled
veneer
of social niceness
and societal niceties –
her cry
was shrill
and indignant.

What?
I've not been invited to the christening?

Showing her sharp wolf-like canines,
she *spat* at the child…

A curse upon you, Aurora.
A curse upon you and your new life
freshly birthed into the world.

For the sins of your parents,
for their sin of omission,
I besmirch your soul
and blacken your being
with a curse
from old days and old ways.

I will steal away from you
that most precious of gifts –
the ability to love
wholeheartedly,
without reserve
or reservation.

I will cast you from
that place of innocence
and newborn delight
of trusting in the world.

You will be mine, Aurora.

I will hold you in thrall
to the black angel
of lovelessness,
I will poison you with the poison
of my own dark soul.

I will steal from you your light
and keep it as my own.

No! spoke Aurora.
You do not have the power
to steal
from me
that which I hold
deep within
that pervades my soul
and flows in my veins
and breathes my breath for me.

Your curse is empty
and sows no seed
and bears no fruit
in the fertile soil of my being.

This curse is yours –
not mine
never mine –
to own
and to wear
and to carry as your burden
as it scratches you to pieces
from within
as it turns your skin to scales
and your heart to stone.

As I turn my back
and walk away
and grow new skin
and birth new dreams
into my lighter
into my brighter
world.

2019

* This poem references Carabosse's curse on Sleeping Beauty in Tchaikovsky's version of the fairy tale. It also deals with the psychic damage that a vengeful being attempts to inflict on another. 'Curse' is dedicated to those who have been abused and traumatised by others, whether it be by individuals, families or by society. May you set yourself free from those who are uncaring, unloving and unjust in their treatment of you.

Dark Imaginings

Dark imaginings
come like thieves in the night
creeping on soft-soled shoes
intent on dark and dastardly deeds
hell-bent on hateful and mean needs.

Dark and dire imaginings
with nefarious purposes
creeping on soft-soled shoes
testing if the door is locked
tapping on windows
forcing entry inside
seeking soul-theft.

Little knowing
my soul is not theirs for the stealing
not theirs for the reeling
in like fish thrown
bloody burley.

Nor is it for sale
nor do I give my soul away
not even if they ask nicely
which they never do.

Dark and deceptive imaginings
creeping on soft-soled shoes
outside my house
silent and breathing shallow breaths
behind the door
of my morning mind
ever present
alongside my mourning mind
which sees only loss
and is lost
always so lost
because you left.

Dark and devious imaginings
are akin to the false friends
who steal your soul
steal your time
steal your faith
steal your trust
in your own self
and in human kind
in that oh-so-lovely kindness of humankind.

My soul protects my heart
my heart protects my soul
from dark imaginings
old and primordial imaginings
ancient and antediluvian imaginings
since before the Flood
rising up from the depths
of my soul
under this full and fulsome moon
where tides ebb and flow
first high and then low
and dark imaginings
creep away softly
on soft-soled shoes

2023

Dearall

If I am to honour this day
as the newborn she is
emerging shyly
quietly
into the late afternoon of my life
not yet twilight
not quite…

If I am to welcome this newborn day
unto my breast and suckle her
feeding her
with soft words
that coo like doves
who find shelter
in the cool eves of churches
in the bright heat of day…

If I am to nurture this brand new day
that ages as I write
words
that wend their way
out of my body
birthed by my soul
into the heart of this
early morning day
into the soul of this soft morn…

Will she love me back?

Will we love each other
as we both age
through this day
through time
of new morn
new dawn
to this one day passing
to yesterday passed by
walking away
as you did
on that long ago
dawn of time
at that birth of a new age?…

Will we love each other
as if you – this new bright and shiny day –
will never come again
will never again appear on my horizon
moving slow-oh-so-slow
like the soft caress of a lover's hand
across the land
of our lives?…

Can we love each unto the other
and move soft
gentle
through time
this allotted time
we are given
as gifts
of a great and generous love?…

Hope is that thing with feathers
Emily told us
speaking true
of this new love between this new day
and I…

Hope springs eternal
my mother often told me
in every human breast.

Hope lies low and quiet
at the bottom of
Pandora's box
and moves alongside
this new day and I.

Yes, we will love each other
and on one new day
after this newborn day today
we will look back with fondness
at this newest of new beginnings
at this dawning of this new day…

2023

Do Middle-aged Men Travel On Buses?

Do they get a shock
when some bright young thing,
well brought-up
and well-meaning,
stands
and offers
…ohgodnoplease…
with the deference and courtesy
due to one of such advanced years
their seat?

Or is the illusion
of the middle-aged man
with his red sports car
and his teenaged companion
only supportable
if you never
travel on buses,
and are never accosted
by polite youth
showing you the deference
due your age?

2009

Down the Bunny Hole

Down the bunny hole
I trip and I tumble…

Lured by the unknown
the mystery
sparkling in the darkling
glittering in the gloaming
fairy dust twinkling
with soft quiet pink
and grace given
shedding some light on the matter
showing softer quieter tones
softer quieter ways and means
softer quieter dreams and schemes…

Dark things and light things
unicorns and horned toads
escaped from witches brew
making and breaking
and shapeshifting
betwixt and between
the light and the dark
and all…
so-many…
shades in between
lightening and darkening
tones and nuance and subtleties
enlightenment and endarkenment…

Shadows passing overhead
darkening the moment
just this moment
this one brief and tiny nanosecond
from this great and wondrous infinity of time
spread wide in the sky
arms outstretched
ready to catch me if I fall…

Shadows pass
clouds part
sun shines through
breaks through gloom
breaks down barriers
breaks through resistance
breaks my silence
with relentless
quiet joy.

2022

Epidermic Growth

Eucalypts –
those sparse
spindly
tall and towering
trees
we like to own
as uniquely ours
but that I find in the
forests of Spain
to remind me of home
to call me back home
with their sweet clean scent.

Grey-green gums
whose graceful leaves
suckle koalas
who die
in their thousands
their tens of thousands
their small paws
burned
their fur
singed
the sickly smell of
their poor charred flesh.

Nature's will to live
despite us
the epidermic growth
of eucalypts
after fire has burned all to ash
copper-pink leaves sprout
soft and fragile
the colour of
a koala's tongue
tender
as a lost lover's embrace
fresh
as new skin
that grows
over old wounds.

2020

I wrote this in response to the horror of the 2020 bushfires. The title was inspired by a conversation I heard on the radio as I was driving back from Victoria, when the landscape was still smoking, people beside the highway cheering the RFS as they sirened their way to fires. An environmentalist was speaking about the signs of hope, of regrowth that would naturally – that is, as part of nature – occur after some time. I misheard 'epicormic' as 'epidermic'. Thanks, Jeannie Lawson, for the correction. But I'll leave it as it is, because the colour is so true – the connections between gum leaves and koala paws and human skin are so true.

Fear is leaving now

Fear is leaving now,
sneaking away
in the early hours of the morning
like a cowardly lover
who promised the earth
and heaven on earth
and long slow mornings
leaking into languor-filled days.

Fear opens the door quietly
knowing how to lift it slightly
on its hinges
to stop the squeak
from waking me
out of my tranced sleep.

I open one eye
and my sleepy dream-dry eyelid
squeaks slightly
startling fear
at the door
his hand on the doorknob
one foot on the threshold
of being here
the other on the verge
of being there.

He looks back at me
furtive
and guilty
and practised
and cowardly.

A small-hearted lover
not worthy of my time
or the giving up of my days
or the fixing of my squeaky hinges.

2015

Feet in the Sand, Head in the Clouds…

Feet shuffling deliciously,
light as air,
skimming and skipping
through gold-grained sand,
plowing furrows over dunes.

Brown feet,
shuffling slow,
weaving plaits,
making grooves.

Light, tiny feet,
airlight, airbright, sunbright,
rippling over sand.

Feet planted firmly,
head in the clouds,
feet on the ground,
in the sand.

Golden grains of sharp light,
glittering in the sun's rays,
patterns over water,
like stones cast,
light as clouds in a blue blue sky,
startling white in a blue blue sky.

Yellow-gold circles,
tiny as fleas,
clasped in my hands,
and my heart bouncing over ripples.

My head in the clouds,
soaring, flying,
head in the clouds,
heart in my hands,
my feet
on the ground,
in the sand.

1998

For God, King and Country

For God, King and Country
intones the stone memorial
at the local cricket ground
    …they died.

I read the names
carved in grey stone
once chiselled in sharp relief
now muted by time and weather.

A tiny snail
moves across the grey stone
slithering its silver trail behind
over the names
of those
who died
For God, King and Country.

A small, cheerful sparrow
alights on the cold stone monument
hopping across the top
pecking at the silver trail
shining over the names
of those who died.

A dry, brown leaf
flutters from the naked branches
of an old old tree
overhanging the cold grey slab
with its long-dead names
wreathed with its trail of silver.

A nest of brown curling leaves
gathers at the foot of the stone memorial
a light autumn blanket of leaves
covering the cold dead feet
of those who died
    …in the name of Peace.

1998

From the Shadow Lake

From the shadow lake
drunk as a wind symphony
dreaming with blue white sleep
under vision and eternity
beneath mist on your mad wet skin
essential
so languid
she watches love.

2007

Ghosts of Christmas Past

When Auntie Trish said, 'No more!
Why should I be the only one
who – year after year –
performs this odious chore?'

All aghast and agog,
mouths hanging open
in Silly Season surprise,
the rellies…looked at the dog.

'Who to kick?' they asked,
bebothered and bewildered.
'Poor Auntie Trish?
Or the dog who sits there equally aghast?'

Three brothers, one sister,
separated quite young,
the brothers and their families
left Christmas to Trish and it really pissed her.

'Enough!' said Auntie Trish
'I'm shutting up my shop.
You'll have to take your Chrissy elsewhere,
I've made my final wish.'

2013

Good Catholic Girls

We went to see the priest – Father Duffy was his name.
Six of us good Catholic girls, we crossed the road, we were game.
We giggled a little, but not very much –
giggling was for state school girls and we were not such.

Knocking brightly at the door, we were ushered inside
to the inner sanctuary, full of sunshine and spiritual pride.
A question for Father Duffy and we were up next,
not one of a spiritual nature – we wanted to know about sex.

Why is it wrong, Father, we had to ask,
To…well…you know…phew! what a task.
We giggled, we stammered and then we blushed –
we good Catholic girls, we models of hush.

Father Duffy smiled, he probably knew what was coming
from a good Catholic school, where sex was fairly humming.
No need to be afraid, girls, Father Duffy called,
I'm God's representative and *He's* seen it all!

Five good Catholic girls looked at me, for I had been elected
to ask this oh so tricky question that we had selected.
Petting, Father, I said with a burst,
why's it so wrong and how can it hurt?

Father Duffy didn't seem surprised and he didn't look shocked
at such a controversial question from six of his flock.
Well, girls, he said with understanding cool,
(a priest of the new order, this one, and in no way a fool)
sex is like a swimming pool.

A swimming pool! we thought, all us eager little swimmers,
deep and dark and wet, full of tiny spermy skimmers.
Giggling and squirming, we waited for more
of Father Duffy's unusual reading of God's law.

We good Catholic girls waited breathless in anticipation
for a continuation of this new and latest revelation.
Do you get just as wet in the shallow end, Father Duffy asked,
as when you dive head-first into the very deepest part?

Our heads still full of tiny spermy skimmers, we nodded with
glee, all us eager little swimmers.
At last Father Duffy looked just a wee bit surprised,
his anti-sex lesson wasn't being read as he'd surmised.

Before Father Duffy could clear up this spiritual misunderstanding,
we good Catholic girls, all prim and proper and all very randy,
raced to the door with good Catholic poise –
we were off to teach swimming to the good Catholic boys.

And these days, I must say that all us good Catholic girls
as enthusiastic swimmers are well known throughout the world.
So we thank you Father Duffy, for those words so long ago
of swimming pools and wetness and diving with the flow.

1995

Hardening of the Hearteries

A harder heart
is necessary to survive
in a hard world.

But it is something to be guarded against.

A softer heart
is necessary to survive
with joy
in a hard world.

It is something to be guarded and protected.

2008

Hardly Ever Drowning

Watching two small dots
in the waves
one with arm up-stretched
waving or drowning or just swimming
impossible to tell from this distance…

One moving closer to shore
one with her back turned
looking out to the far horizon
the not so far bombora
wave after wave crashing onto
its small distant rocky shore
surging high into the sky…

Spatial recognition possible
facial recognition impossible
from this distance
sitting on hard grey concrete
watching murky brown waters
turbulent and tossed
around and about…

Surrounding two small dots
one with arm now descended
neither waving nor drowning
the other now turned towards shore
farseeing eyes now watching more closely
now seeing more finely…

Muddy brown silt from the Hawkesbury River
suspended in murky Pacific Ocean waters
making visibility difficult
true sight clouded
inner sight
turned inwards
concerned
about keeping head above water
and hardly ever drowning…

Raising arm upwards
into air…

2022

He Sculpted Her In Sand

He sculpted her in sand on the beaches of his youth
he took sand from the desert to sculpt her shape
he moulded her from garden clay and river mud
thick and dark and slippery
he fired her soul in lava pools and volcanic heat.

He sculpted her in sand on the beaches of his life
when he was a small child and later
as a slender adolescent.
And he sculpted her in sand in the deserts of his life
when he was older and wandered the world
and was weary of the world.

He sculpted her from the stone
that formed the steep mountain sides
that he climbed
and then tumbled back down
like Sisyphus with his boulder.

He smoothed her rough and pointy spots
with gentle hands and soft touch
with rhythmic movements of his work-roughened palms
sliding away straight lines
creating curls and curves.

He fired her form in the lava
that flowed from volcanic eruptions.
He anointed her with warm oil on her golden skin
and spilled starlight on her sleepy eyelids.

And he painted her
coloured her
with all the colours of the rainbow.

He ate cubes of mango off her golden skin,
his sharp teeth nipping at the tender flesh
as if it were a precious, extra-tasty part of her
succulent and golden
mango-flavoured and delicious,
light and life-giving.

And he made her come into the World
even before she was born
was birthed
was fully formed and fully firmed into herself
into her own True Being.

He made her come into the World.
He made her come.

And they were linked forevermore
for all time
from time eternal
from the first Adam and Eve
God and his Serpent
Jesus and Mary Magdalene.

They were linked together
and he breathed life into her
as he kissed her wetly
sensuously
on her still dry and lifeless mouth.
He injected spirit and sperm into her
gave her moisture with his tongue
and his mouth
and his fingers.

Even in death were they linked
even when one lived and breathed
while the other rotted in a worm-eaten casket
in the dark, mouldering recesses of mother Earth
were they linked unto each other.

2001

How

This is how much i love you...
as wide as my child's arms
stretched wide
from furtherest-reach finger tip
to furtherest-reach finger tip
from the top of the hill
way down
to the bridge over the creek
at the bottom of our street.

This is how i remember you...
easy,
ahhhh longest-sigh so easy
so easy
i bring you
back from the dead
and call you into my mind
to sit beside me again
and i tell you all my woes
all my confusion
now that my world
encompasses more
than from the top of the hill
way down
to the wooden bridge
that rattles when we drive over it
that spans the creek
at the bottom of our street.

This is how i will heal you…
with words
of deepest-reach solace
that soothe my soul
you say to me
if they clip your wings
or crush your petals
if they bruise your pride
or betray you with lies
it's their loss
my sad little friend
it's their
furtherest longest deepest-reach
loss.

2015

I Have Lived Long

I have lived long enough to understand
that I do not need all the answers
in order to speak out
out of the mouths of babes.

That I do not need all the answers
as I sit beneath my cornflower blue skies that speak to me
out of the mouths of babes
and paint invisible pictures of dancers.

As I sit beneath my cornflower-blue skies that speak to me
my long life is loud inside my white noise mind
and I paint invisible pictures of dancers
that move as clouds from within.

My long life is loud inside my white noise mind
it lulls me into a sweet afternoon swoon
that moves as clouds from within
into the bright world without certainty.

Without any need for bright and shiny certainty
I have lived long enough to understand
that I have no necessity for deep-rooted rightness
in order to speak out.

2016

I Have Seen People Create

I have seen people create
Joy out of Sorrow…

A beautiful young man,
quite unaware of his magnificence,
who created dance and unity
and a brief moment of delight in a busy city.
He created joy for others
from his own sorrow for his brother
who died only three weeks after being diagnosed
with leukaemia.

I have seen people create
Beauty out of Anger…

A young woman,
both loving and hating
her alcoholic father.
She creates for the world a vision
of a wedding veil,
white and voluminous
and full of promise.
Hooked and snagged and caught in the veil
are tiny fishing lures, pretty and feathered
and full of colour
to represent the allure of the feminine.

I have seen people create
sweet nectar from their tears,
find prisms of light and colour
in the depths of their sadness,
in the shadows of their fear.

I have seen the most unlikely materials
made into Moments of Bright Life.

2009

I Painted the Sky Last Night

Last night I followed the contours of the coast
from Bronte to Bondi.
I carried a can of house paint with me
and a thick, heavy brush.

As I followed the lines of the coast,
the sun began to set
and the sky became a ceiling
of pastel pinks and blues
stretching in front and around and above me.

But I wanted more –
more colour, more vibrancy,
more connection with Creation.

So I plunged my brush
into the can of house paint
and slapped it across the sky –
giant brush strokes of thick paint
in swathes of glorious colour.

I saw people stop to admire
my sky of rose-pink, dusty-plum, fuchsia,
my clouds of slate-grey and deep blue,
like volcanic eruptions in the sky.

I saw one man walking with his face upturned,
awash in sky colours,
as if the paint had been too heavy, too vibrant
to remain in the sky
and had leaked earthwards
and clothed him in sunset.

2015

In the End Times

This is what every old person knows…
that in the end, they will lie.

That by the time they are old
they will have sold their souls
each for what mattered
most
at the time
    ambition
    money
    family
    ease and comfort.

Sacrificing one for the other
    passion for peace
    swords for ploughshares
    allies for enemies
    and then back again.

They will lie as they lay dying
they will not want their children
to know too much of the truth
too soon.

That life is harsh
that they are cruel
that it is not only nature
which is sharp of tooth and claw
that they too
have tracked and brought down and skinned and eaten alive

their enemies
their workmates
their colleagues-in-arms
their neighbours
their loved ones
their husbands their wives
their brothers their sisters
their children
the children of their children.

They sowed seeds of division
in divided times
divisive times
dividing dimes and pennies and cents on the dollar
they sold their souls
for peanuts
traded their souls
for beans.

I told you to buy a goat, Jack!
with our pitiful few and pitiful precious
pennies
and you return from the market
that place of soul-trading
Jesus in the marketplace
with his whip
and his fury
at commerce
conducted
in his Father's house

power shuffles and power deals and power trades
and power wins
and you bring me back
a handful of beans.

Old men, old women
throwing bodies
of young men, young women
onto funeral pyres
of endless wars
harpies
descending from blackening skies
smoke-filled
and poisoned
scorched earth policies
White Australia policies
education policies and environment policies and tax policies
and health care policies
political policies
and politics making strange bedfellows indeed
with filthy cum-smeared sheets and filthy grimy hands and
filthy dirty deals.

But in the end times
in our marking-of-time and our making-of-time
in our soul-trading
and deal-making
and promise-breaking

there are also
small children
making cards to send to strangers
and thereby making new friends
and neighbours making food
there are markets of home-made things
that bring riches beyond wildest dreams
new dreams
and new truths
and truth-telling
that come because they need to come
to give the lie to the lie
that innocence has died
is weak
is feeble
is powerless
and we sow seeds of peace
to grow some justice
in our new gardens.

2021

Just Because

When they asked me why
I told them…

Because I love the sea
and because I love waves on the shore
because I love the sound of rain on the roof
and I love to see water running in the gutters

Because I love open doors on a summer night
and autumn leaves falling from the trees
because I love the naked branches of winter
and I love the flowers of springtime

Because I love bright kites flying in the park
and because I love the city lights at night
because I love the noise and colour of the markets
and the bustle of life in the streets

Because I love music and singing
because I love good food
because I love books
because I love dogs and sometimes, cats

Because I love the sound of your laughter
and I love the stillness and the silence
because I love the song of the sea
and the sigh of the wind
and the cry of seagulls in flight

Because I'm stubborn
because I'm brave
because I'm determined

Because I love life

Just Because…

1998

Kissing You

I will kiss you like there is no tomorrow.

Tomorrow will have flown
fled into the future by the time
that far distant moment in time
when you stop kissing me
has been and gone, long gone
has arrived and left
with the speed of light
and the sound of light
and unbearable lightness of being
bouncing between your lips
and mine.

The sun will have risen and set,
both dawn and dusk
will have said bonjour and au revoir.

The moon and the sun
will have kissed
hello and goodbye
at the edge of the horizon,
in a burst of red flame
or a subtle shower
of pastels and rainbows,
of rainwater on newborn flowers.

By the time
your mouth
leaves my mouth,
the Universe
will have died out
and recreated itself,
born from the union –
of your mouth on mine.

2004

Know & Tell

That special place reserved in Hell
for those who know but do not tell
who sacrifice children on this day today
and again on the…good morrow to you
my good man, my gentle good woman
my fellow hypocrites…
that quick switch from Dr Jekyll to Mr Hyde
who both of them know but do not tell
and no, I will not go gentle into that good night
my good sir, my most esteemed madam.

Nor will I allow *you* to go silent
and pretend innocence and unknowing
as you sacrifice another child
another boy another girl
another man woman sister brother
and pretend that you did not know
and still you refused to tell.

That deep and dark pit of despair
bottomless terrifying ground-giving-way
earth-given-away to the highest bidder
that extra-special place in Hell
that I reserve just for you
all pretence all falsehood all disappearing-act
all bluster no substance all sturm und drang
all talk no action all hat no cattle.

I bequeath unto you
quicksand that brings slow and painful death
each moment of your last moments
you mindful of
each grain of sand each molecule of water
shifting and sliding
sidling sideways
like a corrupt and greedy politician
a priest a bishop a pope a nun
who plays God and betrays God
and destroys children's lives
young children old children
who knows names could name names but does not tell.

He and she and they
who should be defrocked unfrocked
– shoulda coulda woulda –
stripped naked and cast to the wolves
hung drawn and quartered
tarred and feathered
bamboo shoved under fingernails
exquisitely slow exquisitely painful
sending nerves singing
to that special place in Heaven
where agony meets ecstasy
where St Teresa of Avila meets her Beloved
where flesh is mortified but spirit and soul release.

For you who know but do not tell
I wish for you that very special place in Hell
with the pure unbridled hatred of an untamed child
wounded and hurt and snarling and biting
…don't hurt me don't touch me don't touch me don't hurt me…

I blow on my dandelion seed head and I wish for you
waterboarding
simulated drowning again and again
enhanced interrogation techniques applied
to make you say out loud
what you know but do not tell.

I wish for you all the torments and night terrors
the cries of abandoned children
screaming and then silent
of dead soldiers and civilians
of destroyed forests and burning towns
of rising sea levels and drowned refugees
to wake you in fright in the dead of the night

I wish for you
long sleepless nights of guilt and shame and
self-recrimination
from your conscience born
of reaping rewards from knowing but not telling.

2022

Minutes

And what will I do with this bright and shiny new day?
this delicious and delightful new day?
These 1440* minutes
all so distinct, so different
from yesterday's portion
of God-given
and God-willing-that-I-don't-die-today
– so far so good –
minutes.

Each one rising like a new sunrise
each setting like a new sunset
each one incorporating the Universe in a grain of sand
each grain held in my hand
– open and receptive
ready to receive –
the grace and the blessings of this one bright moment
like the communion host
from the hand
of the small-town, tiny-town, tidy-town priest
who – from best recollection –
wasn't a small-town, tiny-town, tidy-town
child-molesting, paedophile priest.

Not all were.
Phew!
So blessed, so lucky.
Not all were –
either blessed or lucky.

This first minute so muddled
still half-asleep in Frog Pyjamas
– wondering where on earth Tom Robbins
got *that* phrase from
so quirky, so strange, so beguiling –
stumbles to the kitchen
kickstarts the day with coffee
wonders with half its muddled mind
about starting up a kickstarter fund
or maybe starting up a start-up.

This second minute
so distinguished
so proud
so standing tall
so separate
from this minute just passed
passed away
dead and gone
dead in the water
now deceased
like Monty Python's parrot.

This third minute
rising up from its knees
separating from the herd
flying free from the flock
unweighted down by expectations
of being the same minute as the last minute
of being the same day as yesterday's day
or the same person as another person.

This fourth minute
when the penny drops
finally.

This fifth minute
solid and substantial
in its own presence
when pennies fall from heaven
and are placed on the closed eyes
of the dead.

This sixth minute.

2023

It's taken me more than thirty years since those strange days indeed in Kathmandu, where synchronicities fell from the sky and, like Icarus, so did I, to realise that the allusion to 1,440 sunsets in St Exupéry's *Le Petit Prince* was to do with the 1,440 minutes in a day. A university education never goes astray.

My Secret Love of Spindrift

When my secrets are all told
when I am old
    when I hold fast to the truth
        and thereby loose my fast holding
        of this one swift moment
            of the truth
        scurrying
            from me
as it chases spindrift
        running fast and far
    before wind and sea

        that meet and embrace
        and hold me in arms
    of blue and white and mist and right
    of spray and air and crest and prayer
of lead grey   and iron grey   and steel grey
of pockets full
of water-wet
        black slippery stones

that weight me down
    as I step into the swift-flowing current
        my secrets spill from me
unbidden
    unheld-back
    like spray blown from the crests of waves
        by the wind
    water turned into mist atop waves
            blown
        like scraps of paper
holding truths
    that disappear
        and disintegrate

        as quickly as they are told…

2015

Spindrift: spray blown from the crests of waves by the wind; driving snow or sand. Origin: early seventeenth century (originally Scots): variant of spoondrift, from archaic spoon 'run before wind or sea' + the noun drift.

Ocean Mist

Ocean mist
swirls in,
curls in,
like smoke,
from the bay.

Carried
by fingers of light
over sun-dappled
ocean.

2013

Pitcher Plants and Pitfall Traps*

with thanks to David Attenborough

And how will I save myself this morning?

I will use my lifeline into the past –
    Be thankful for small mercies,
    be grateful for small miracles,
        my mother often told me.

So I give thanks
that I'm not the hapless fly
an unfortunate passerby
supping sweet nectar
at the lip of the pitcher plant
all abuzz with pleasure and delight
all innocent, not yet forlorn
celebrating my good luck
not giving a fuck
thanking Beelzebub –
my Lord of the flies –
for my great happenstance
doing my little happy dance
on the lip of the pitcher plant.

That slippery slope
all bright-coloured
and narrow-ridged
and sweet nectar-laden
coated with smooth wax
too smooth for even the hairy legs
of the grateful, thanks-giving fly
to grab hold
to hold within its grasp
its footing on the slippery slope
the bright-coloured
enticing
pheromone-laden
lip of the pitcher plant.

Little pitchers have big ears
my sainted mother also said
my sainted mother now long dead
Saint Mum
– as I once ruefully said –
to my not-yet-sainted Dad
who was not-yet dead.

The fly, scrabbling madly for a foothold,
slips
– inevitably –
into the open maw below
full with flesh-dissolving liquid
rich in enzymes
ever-waiting, ever-ready

to receive unto itself
another sacrifice
live and sated
with food
free-given
left at the threshold
on the slippery lip
of the ever-generous pitcher plant.

Live and sated with sweet nectar
but now sad and fat with regret
the fly looses its hold
loses its grip
on its reality
free falls into the abyss
dissolves into its bliss –
Saint Fly
Saint Beelzebub –
both saint and sinner
human-like in this manner
in these matters
of life and of death.

2022

* The tropical pitcher plant, or nepenthes, is a highly complex and refined bug catcher. They are carnivorous plants that eat insects, trapping them using modified leaves known as pitfall traps, which are vase-shaped and filled with nectar that acts as a digestive fluid. Prey is drawn into the pitcher traps and digested by the plant's enzymes.

The Pheromone of Love Meets the Scent of Sex

Scented with the pheromone of love,
    with the scent of sex,
        with the music of muscles –
            …tensed,
                …and tight,
                    …and taut,
                        …and taunting.

With the sounds and the sighs of the senses,
    and scented with the pheromone of love,
        and the scent of sex,
            …the sighs of sex,
                …the sounds of sex,
                    …the smiles of sex,
                        …the slyness of sex.

Drowning in the water and wine,
    swimming in space and time,
        we move to the rhythm of sex,
            …and the flow of love,
                …and the fluids of sex,
                    …and the knowing of love,
                        …and the noises of sex,
                            …and the joy
                    …and the laughter

    …of Love,
        …and of Sex.

2000

Record Keeping

And if you come to me all innocent and forlorn
all regretful and torn
between the rightery and the wrongery
gathered in your multitudes
in that field of Rumi's
much trampled in the dust
made muddy by rain
quicksand in its terrain
and you beseech unto the Heavens
I didn't know I didn't knooooow.

Arms raised in supplication
begging for your life your way of life your lifestyle
we didn't know we didn't knoooooow
shower your mercy down upon us –
oh Lord, oh God, oh giver of Salvation.

Knees made bloody
as you crawl over sharp granite and
drybones deadbones tinybones
of those you sacrificed
all the lives you stole
made small insignificant like we didn't matter at all.

We didn't know we didn't knooooow.

Yes, you did, you liar you defrauder you defiler
you with no dignity no honour no truth no rights –
I offer you no respect no mercy.

You knew
we told you
and here's the evidence
mountains of evidence
the chain of evidence
decades of evidence
forests of trees turned to paper
all piled high in Rumi's field
where rightery and wrongery finally prevail
where witches burn on pyres
maddened by fire
point scornful fingers
and whisper with harsh long-dead voices –
you knew and you were silent.

Ohdeargod!
you cry again
up into the heedless Heavens
she knows she knooooooows
as sand grains separate from water molecules
and slip sideways
as you sink more slowly
than immortal time itself
into quicksand
a death slower and more frightening
than waterboarding
slow drowning
that you invented
to bring truth into the world

but no, not this truth
harsh and sharp and merciless
dead skeletal fingers pointing at you
old people's fingers children's fingers
bony fingers of dead friends dead family
pointing at you –
and you and you and you.

Because you knew you knew.
We told you.
And here's the evidence.

2022

Pockets

I keep falling into pockets full of love
emptying pockets full of lint
love – like lint –
hidden away in the folds
and corners
of life.

Difficult to get rid of
tricky to obliterate
like troublesome
weeds that invade a garden.

A garden of serenity
and non-attachment
serene and detached
not messy and mismatched.

2009

Requiem for Eagles

Requiem.
Origin Middle English:
from Latin –
accusative of *requies* 'rest'
requiescat in pace.
pronunciation: '*re-kwee-es-kaht in pah-che*'
translation: 'may he (or she)

(or they)
(or I)
(or we)
rest in peace.'
May we *all* rest in peace.

May we rest in peace,
be in peace,
live in peace,
before we
die in peace,
and rest in peace,
requiescat in pace
some more.

Eagles:
The greatest of birds,
of majesty,
of grace,
playing with the wind,
swooping down
from on high
to prey on field mice
and paddock rats
and other small burrowing animals,
praying with them
for brief moments
before death
is delivered
by beak and claw,
tiny bones crushed and broken.

2013

A Small Kindness

What small kindness can I do today
on this early morn
this dark before dawn
when we both awaken
to this one fine day?

I can remind us both
us two
that there will come that day
that certain day
when we both
lie dead on this battlefield
of you win/I lose
this dusty plain
of Rumi's
bloodied like the plains of Sparta.

When we meet on that day
where there is only loss
and losers
who have long ago
tossed their last
pair of dice
Leela laughing
at how little learned
in such long lifetimes.

Each die strewn by long-dead gamblers
like dead white rose petals
on flat green baize
with none of the softness
underfoot
of soft soles of bare feet
treading on the soul
of our Earth
none of the undulating gentleness
the undiluted kindness
of small gestures of greeting
and welcoming each other
to this one fine day.

2023

Smatterings

'What do you do?'

A simple question
or so one would imagine
cast across the table at lunchtime
on a world weary
rain-heavy
slow and simple
Covid day.

'Hmmm,' I wonder to mygoodself,
'What indeed *do* I do?'

'A transpersonal art therapist?'
they muse
across the table back to you.
'What's that?'…

Transpersonal:
going beyond matter, beyond the ego, that which is created.
or Created…
much more use of Capital Letters
in the Transpersonal World – big T, big W (but no, not the supermarket)
than in the material world – little m, little w.

Art:
the expression or application of human creative skill and
imagination…producing works to be appreciated primarily for
their beauty or emotional power.

Therapist:
a person skilled in therapy; treatment intended to relieve or heal a disorder:
Origin: mid-nineteenth century: from Greek therapeia 'healing', from therapeuein 'minister to, treat medically'.

Minister:
attend to the needs of someone; provide something necessary or helpful.

'A material anthropologist?' they echo back to you,
'What's that?'…
with a slight air of bemusement
a quizzical wondering
at a box not quite fitting
a box not ticked
hand hesitating over the invisible
intangible
checklist of the lunchtime chat.

'Hmmm,' I wonder to mygoodself,
'What *is* that?'

Material:
relating to matter, that which is made.

Anthropology:
the study of human societies and cultures and their development.

Material anthropology:
studying something which has been made by the hands of
another to gain insights.
What guided those hands,
what society and culture guided that heart, that soul, that spirit
to make something out of thin air and turn it into matter,
a thing that matters and speaks…volumes…
and tells tales upon tales, stories upon stories,
weaving together the day and the night, yesterday, today and tomorrow,
binding together the broken bits, the torn apart parts,
touching gentle with soft hands the wounds and the bruises.

'What do I do?'
I think
I try and help people
via their words and their images
the makings
of their soul
from that deeper well within
so that
neither of us drown
in deep waters
and we emerge
more whole
more filled up to the brim
with beauty
and with wonder
on rainwet
soft and slow
Covid days.

2020

Walking's Enjoyment is Three Level Vision

I would respectfully suggest
    …put forward,
        …move, perhaps,
that walking's enjoyment
is multi-levelled,
multi-hued,
multi-layered vision
with the built-in potential for
sixth sense seeing.

I would respectfully
    …motion
that teaching the body
to see once more
could
    …begin, perhaps,
        …one step at a time,
            …moving-ever-so-slowly
with walking's enjoyment.

Track sustainable:
    …rock, roots and circular wood rounds
disperse water,
track thus meanders,
ensuring a slower pace.

Life sustainable:
    …falls, trips and lostness in the woods
disperse time.

Mind and heart,
    ...soul and spirit
thus meander,
ensuring a sweeter pace.

The partially blind white native tip moth
that changed the course of the trunk of the tree
enabling it
to work with
    ...move with
        ...see with
the vision of another
native.

2013

When Death Comes

When Death comes,
let Him come gently, let Him speak kindly.

When Death comes for me,
may He come softly like a small wave
arriving at the shore from the vast endless ocean.

Let Him
walk beside me for a time like a friendly dog
walking with His master at Dawn.

When Death is with me,
may He be as light as a feather on the breath of God,
as light as a dandelion seed in the hand of its maker.

Let Him come to me
like the lion lying down with the lamb –
at peace with each other, side by side.

When Death comes for me
may we offer each other the Sign of Peace
and smile into each other's hearts.

When Death comes to me,
let us become friends for a while
so that we may know each other
before I go with Him.

Let Death come to me
like an old friend I haven't seen for a long time.

Let Death speak to me
of my family who He keeps in His care and who miss me.

Let Death
not take away the laughter I have shared with friends,
and may my friends remember our laughter together
when I have gone.

When Death comes for me
let Her come lovingly like a Mother come to collect Her child
when he is tired and ready to come home from play.

When Death takes me,
may She take me with love
and may I leave love behind me in the world.

When I am with Death,
may the world be richer that I have lived
and poorer that I have passed.

2010

A Woman and Two Candles

And herein lies a tale
that waits to be told,
    that needs to be told,
        that asks to be told
of a woman and two candles –
one burning brightly while the other grows cold.

A step into the future.

Poised on the cliff,
the past floats around her,
silent voices of the dead and the gone,
refusing to die,
    refusing to live whole,
        unable to let go,
            unable to move on.

Fear builds upon fear,
the future is both far and both near
    but the present is here.

Paper tigers dance
and look at her askance.

What is a future,
    without a past?
        they ask.
What is now –
    without you,
        without thou?

She lights the cold candle –
the past comes alive
its flame flickers bright –
paper tigers recede
    into the night.

She changes one for the other –
    the past for the future,
        the future for the past.

Both blend together,
    both will grow cold
        as she will grow old.

No candle for the present.

It burns as she writes
    in the night
        by the light

Of the candle of the past
    and the candle of the future
        and the pen of the present.

2000

The Woman Called God

There once was a woman
who called herself God.

She went by other names of course,
being called sister by some,
friend by others,
mother by a few
and fool by many.

But as lover she was known to none.

So, one day,
out of her loneliness and her need,
    she created man.

The man she created
was a reflection of herself
and so she called him God, as well.

He, too, was known by other names –
brother, friend, father and fool.

The main divide between them was that he –
this man, her creation –
    was known as lover to many.

And oh, she loved him immediately,
this creation of hers.

For was he not beautiful in every way,
    and had she not created him
        from the beauty of her own soul
            and the love of her heart
                and the laughter of her spirit?

And was he not so beautiful
    that it was as if he had been formed out of dust
        by the very hand of God?

And so she gave thanks to the power of creation
and tried to put out of her mind,
    the main divide between them –
        that he was lover to many
           and she,
                only lover to he.

But after the passing of one full moon,
the woman called God
realised
that despite her best efforts and her best intentions,
she had created a God
who was unsuited for her needs.

With the passing of one full moon,
she realised that she needed to be set free,
    and that her creation –
        the God she had created
            out of her loneliness and her desire –
                also needed to be set free.

So, when the moon was new again,
a thin sliver of silver in the night sky,
she went in search of her scissors.

They were the scissors she used
for many different forms of cutting –
    the cutting of paper
        and the cutting of cloth
            and the cutting of her own hair
                when it grew a bit straggly and a bit long,
                    obscuring her vision.

And at the beginning of a new day,
when the morning star was still bright in the sky,
she took her scissors and – very deliberately –
cut the cord of creation between them.

And the woman called God
and the man called God
went their separate ways.

He to continue as
>   brother, friend, father, fool
>   >   and lover to many.

And she?
This woman called God?

She gained a deeper respect
>   for the powers of her own creation
>   >   and used them more wisely from then on,
>   >   >   from the full moon to the new
>   >   >   >   and back again.

2001

www.ingramcontent.com/pod-product-compliance
Lightning Source LLC
Chambersburg PA
CBHW071008080526
44587CB00015B/2394